Reset 11:22

The journey of internal healing,
transformation, and redemption.

Martina Common

Reset 11:22 -the journey of internal healing, transformation, and redemption.

Copyright © 2023 by Martina Common

C.A.B.R.I.N.I. Publishing

DEDICATION

I dedicate Reset 11:22 to hurting hearts. So when you feel and are experiencing life challenges, pick this book up for inspiration. I am a living testimony that you can and will make it through if you keep working on YOU and keep the faith.

Reset 11:22

Contents

Code Red

Code Red

If there's such a thing as hell on earth, I resided there. Deadly health scares consumed every waking moment, insecurities altered my appearance, and foreclosure signs rested on my front entrance. I instantly became head of the household while having difficulty accepting my reality: I had always been a single parent. I remained devoted to a man that didn't love me back; old wombs resurfaced from past hardships while closets released dark secrets I could no longer hold back. My friendships were hanging by a thread, and I became the person who had to borrow money without a deadline for returning it. I put my career on hold and lived paycheck to paycheck as I developed a deep hatred for myself. I spent months thinking that I was hiding my pain from my son, who all along could sense something was wrong.

My son was overwhelmed and confused by my daily breakdowns at four years old.

"Don't cry, momma!" he said, staring, misty-eyed, with his little hands shivering as he touched my face.

I couldn't explain to him why his mommy was upset. I couldn't explain to anybody that I wanted out of this thing called life.

I remember riding home from work in a 2-hour commute when bad flashbacks, doubts, fears, anger, sadness, shame, and hatred consumed my thoughts. I was sweating, tearing up, and biting on my lip, not wanting to confess to what I had done too-myself.

Who am I?

Why am I so helpful to people who are not showing me kindness?

Why do I have to sacrifice everything for everyone?

Why am I putting my career on hold?

Why am I raising my child by myself?

Why am I not using my voice?

Why am I not losing weight?

Why is everyone turning their backs on me?

Why am I not at peace?

Why am I not happy?

Why am I here?

I shouted those questions while driving on the bumper-to-the-bumper highway. I punched my horn and put my hand over my mouth to refrain from yelling. I wiped my eyes with my shirt, turned on the air conditioner, inhaled, and exhaled slowly. I glanced before me and saw that the traffic was in snail's motion. Then I looked to my left and froze.

A grey goatee gentleman in the lane to my left observed me crying and yelling the entire time. He continued to stare and looked over his glasses with concern. Then he motioned for me to roll my window down. I continued to stare at him. There was nowhere for me to hide from the shame.

The traffic started to race; I turned around and pressed 20 to 30 mph down the highway. I wiped my face again with my shirt and stared in my rearview mirror, hoping not to see the black BMW following me.

I thought the gray-goatee gentleman knew my secret. A secret that I've kept hidden from everyone. A mystery that put my mind, body, and soul in "code red."

I had hit my version of Rock-Bottom.

I was unhappy with everything. I wasn't living for myself anymore. My creativity had died, and I worked hard to build other people's dreams but not my own.

I continued my drive home in tears. When I pulled into my garage, I took my phone out.

I permanently deleted all social media accounts.

I blocked phone numbers from people who didn't reach out and deleted text messages that would stress me.

Those three things (and more) kept me away from my destiny. I had no one to blame but myself for it.

I CHOSE to let social media and people's "madness" get to me. I consumed myself with

everyone else lives. I would see them living, enjoying their children, building businesses, going on vacation, and making it work with their significant others. I saw them using all the advice, money, and listening ear I had given them. And here I was alone, single, single parent, heartbroken, my account consistently hit negative, my health deteriorating, and I watched my dreams and motivation drop to -*rock bottom*.

I snatched my garage door opener from my sun visor and pulled my car into reverse while watching my garage door shut. I had a choice: to stay inside the running car or go inside my house to my son.

My son was inside the house, awaiting my arrival with open arms and expecting a kiss on his forehead. Instead, I slowly put my hand on the key, took my hand back off, and let the tears fall.

I placed my hand on my chest. And whispered, "I'm sorry."

I put my hand back on the key and turned the car off.

I sat in my car for an hour, crying and wondering how can I get through this. I could see the door to my house swing open from my rearview mirror.

"Momma." my son's cornrows rested on his shoulders.

I wiped my face with my shirt, sat up, and cracked my driver-side door.

My son hopped into my arms; I kissed his forehead, twirled his curly cornrows around my fingers, and squeezed him tight.

I realized that: he deserves his mom: *the real her.*

My son caressed me as I dragged myself out of the car. I avoided eye contact with my mother, standing at the open door. Once inside, I did my nightly motherly duties, read my son his favorite bedtime story, and spent the rest of the night crying. I could hear my mother downstairs repeatedly chanting my name throughout the night, and the gospel tunes of Marvin Sapp were exiting her phone. She had a way of knowing things that needed to be said. And although I was not too fond of that, I loved my mother even more because it kept me safe and spiritually motivated.

I remember my mother losing everything she had worked hard for, and some family members disappeared when we needed them the most. I watched her spend her entire life being a single parent to my sisters and me. And because she could do it, I had the skills to conquer it head-on. But it wasn't the life I wanted for my child and me.

I laid in bed that night, tossing and turning, wondering what was next for me. How could I come back spiritually, mentally, emotionally, and financially? Finally, I got out of bed, checked on my son, could still hear my mother chanting my name throughout her prayer, and grabbed my notebook.

I started writing what you are reading in my diary, which became the foundation of rebuilding my spirit. So, if you are one of the lucky ones that got a chance to get your hands on my first book, A Better Me, then you are very aware of my path, the Hiatus I took, and the growth I embraced; unfortunately, not realizing that silent wounds were still bleeding.

Three things happened to me the night I wanted to take my life inside my car:

1. I realized how broken I was.

2. I realized that I wasn't living my truth.

3. I visualized how heartbroken my son would have been to find his mother's lifeless body.

Number three kept playing throughout my mind. I knew I had to go back to where it all started to overcome this cycle of brokenness: traumatic events during my childhood and painful experiences throughout life that I hadn't healed. Childhood trauma bleeds into adulthood when you don't deal with the pain. It kidnaps your children, significant others, friends, family, and loved ones from being able to enjoy and embrace you fully. And that, to me, is a form of your life in code red. We don't like to admit it, but the cycle continues, and when it does, everything and everyone around you experiences become impacted by it. Emotions, tension, dysfunction, embarrassment, humiliation, jealousy, and pain eat your spirit forever if you don't do the necessary healing work. And I was finally willing to do the job of cleansing and healing even if I had to lose people and things along the way. Who wants to visit a memory, experience, or childhood period where the pain started? NO ONE. Yet, I realized I was not following the path and purpose destined for me because I carried the pain throughout my life. And I was looking at my child, NOT wanting that same childhood for him. Author Lisa Nichols said it best "I was willing to let the old me die, to rebirth the woman I was destined to become." Welcome To My Open Diary Of Healing, Transparency, and Redemption. Welcome to Reset 11:22.

Gem

When dealing with your past once and for all, the poison dies.

Entry 1:
Daddy's Little Girl

Daddy's Little Girl

All my life, I wanted to experience what it feels like to be "Daddy's Little Girl." Sometimes I would sit on my porch waiting for my father, watching every passing car and jumping up when the phone rang. And you want to know what hurts the most. Knowing that it'll never happen. Knowing that my father would never come. My father showed me how deep heartache and disappointment could go, especially from the person who is supposed to be a little girl's first love. In a little girl's eyes, their Dad is the first real model of how a man should treat a woman. My love life revolved around my father's absence, emptiness, embarrassment, and pain. I feared letting go of relationships, and I worked overtime to make it work with previous partners who were unwilling or capable of fighting for and appreciating love, respect, and emotional vulnerability. However, I immediately became aware of the connection. I begged, pleaded, and gave all of me to people who didn't know how to reciprocate unconditional love. I was dating the replicas of my father. I sat down with a notebook and compared/contrasted my father to my previous partners.

My father is not affectionate. The men I've dated aren't either.

My father does not know how to love.

The men I've dated don't either.

My father is broken.

The men I've dated were as well.

And the common thread: men who are hurting.

I compared and contrasted myself to my previous partners.

And the common thread: hurting.

Hurt people. Hurt people.

Absence, lack of bond, and a blurred understanding of the definition of a man and what they are supposed to be resulted in me needing CPR and a better vision. I learned I gave them all love and power while losing my identity and myself. I'm going to repeat it. I needed CPR. And the path to breathing again had to start with forgiveness by going back down the *hurting lane.*

Gem

Embark on the path of forgiveness to live the life you always dreamed of.

Entry 2:

17 years ago

17 years ago

There's an incident over 17 years ago that continues to haunt me. I cringe and cry while thinking about it. I was embarrassed and angry that the man who created me put his hands on me in the most unloving way. It was raining; my friends and I shared umbrellas while walking to the neighborhood chicken spot. Claire, Katie, Katie's cousin Kayla, and I each had pre-ordered our 6-piece chicken meal after practicing for an upcoming talent show. As we walked, laughed, and tried to escape the rain, a black jeep abruptly pulled up in front of us.

"Where are you going? It would be best if you weren't out here!" the firm tone came from the window's crack. Katie and I only knew who the voice belonged to; the others appeared confused and concerned.

"I'm walking to a restaurant for food."

"No, you're not; yall can climb inside this car; I'm taking yall back to the building." Justice had then rolled his window down entirely, and even with his baseball cap on, I could still see the anger in his eyes, reminding me of how nights growing up were like when he hit my mother.

I held onto Katie as we all tried to walk around the car, ignoring him, and he yelled again for me to get in the car. Finally, startled and not wanting my friends to be more afraid, I motioned for us to climb inside, and the doors weren't even closed before he sped off.

Justice was mumbling under his breath as he drove through the rain, sped through yellow lights, and zoomed into the nearby grocery store parking lot. I kept glancing through the rearview mirror to check on my friends, whose eyes were wide and their faces red.

"Do you hear me, Ba-Ba" his voice grew louder.

No one had called me that nickname in years because I didn't want to be called Ba-Ba as a teenager, and he knew that. I could feel my phone vibrating in my left pants pocket, and as I tried to get to it, he shoved my body, with my face hitting the window. My friends gasp in the backseat.

The rain outside had turned into hail, hitting the car and my face.

"Your fast tale was going down there to see some boy," he spat back.

I tried to turn towards him, and Justice shoved me back towards the window again. My face was burning while my friends were crying in the back seat. Justice's voice was still rising, and my eyes continued to open and close. I began to make out-loud banging, with my door opening up abruptly in the midst of this. It was my mother. Screaming, motioning for my friends to exit the car, she held on to me and yelled at Justice.

"You won't strike my kids and me ever again," she slammed his door, shattering the passenger side window.

My friends grabbed hold of me as my mother charged at Justice, with him speeding off. My mother hurried back to me, squeezed me tight, and caressed my face. We stood in the grocery store parking lot for what seemed like hours. No one said anything; we just stared at one another. My friend's lips trembled, my mother wept, and my heart grew colder than the hail falling down.

Seventeen years of my cold heart, I held deep anger towards men; I felt abandoned and hurt by the one who was supposed to protect me from harm, not cause it, and I vowed never to let a man put his hands on me. The pain consumed my entire life, mind and well-being, and self-destruction pattern with men. I thought I had to walk on eggshells to keep the peace, keep someone in my life, and be taken seriously.

What was I thinking?

The examples and images of what Justice had physically, emotionally, and mentally done to my mother, big sister, and I crushed my self-worth, the definition and understanding of what a real man is supposed to be, and the self-value I held for myself.

Women have a natural gift of believing we should fix everything, including people. However, the reality is it is not our job to fix someone.

Say aloud, "it is not your job to fix someone."

You're probably saying it aloud and still don't believe it is not your job. It took me years to say, feel, acknowledge, and live by it.

I thought it was my job to get my father to be in my life, take care of me while growing up, and shower unconditional love. I thought it was up to me not to make Justice angry, silence myself, and close my eyes to the harm and absence. I thought it was my job to rebuild and obey a partner who came into my life, afraid that he would do what my father had done: be cold, disrespectful, and distant if I didn't do what he wanted.

And because I thought this way, I carried an 18-wheeler load of pain throughout my life; it caused me to stop loving myself and caused me to let anything and anybody in, even when the red flags indicated that they shouldn't be in my life. I didn't want to live like that anymore; it was time to shift this mindset. What guided me on this forgiveness journey is realizing that I didn't do anything wrong; Justice's choice to be absent, angry, and violent was HIS choice.

And it became my choice to build healthier boundaries within my heart and soul so that I can be an example to my child of how you conquer adversity. And most importantly, what releasing and healing from pain does for your spirit and purpose in life. So, 17 years ago, this painful childhood memory was the stepping stone to opening the path of forgiveness and positively shifting my mindset for myself, my future, my son, and my sanity.

Gem

Transparency starts from within; once you can get true with SELF, the change for the better starts.

Entry 3:
Transparency

. . . .

Transparency

I can't describe my father's presence in my life because he was not present. Financial assistance was the most I ever got from him back then. Although the financial help was appreciated when Justice provided it, it always came with the price of begging. Imagine someone constantly asking you questions about why you need something after explaining and providing the reason numerous times.

Imagine you being a teenager having to explain to your parent why assistance is necessary for clothing, school supplies, doctor co-pays, and the list goes on.

It's as if he wanted to be rewarded for providing for his children.

"This is what I have done for you," continued to exit his mouth. In my eyes, I didn't believe my mother should be taking care of my sisters and me financially, physically, or emotionally on her own. Justice was alive, financially capable, and able to assist. I stop calling to ask for anything because it shouldn't be hard to get help from your father. I was angry that he would rather see one beg him for it than provide it.

In the present, when I see him doing things for other people, other people's children, and communities, I can't help but wonder if he didn't do anything for his children because my mother left him. You'd be surprised how one action and attitude are taken out on the children when families separate, not realizing the children suffer. Children suffer from feeling neglected by their absent parents and lacking necessities. The present parent is fully providing and is placed in an uphill financial battle to do what the two parents should be supplying, providing, and doing.

For instance, when a child is in preschool and of elementary school age, it's a lot of curiosity rummages through their minds about their life and surroundings. Yet, they get a more transparent dose of reality as they become teenagers and have a clearer and broader understanding of life. So, for example, as a teenager, you see what others have and don't, your friends with both mommy and daddy present, and the reality of what's different or lacking in your life. During my teenage years, this caused emotional frustration and made me feel unworthy due to my father's absence.

Growing up, I never worried or wondered if my mom struggled or needed assistance with anything because there was not one time I didn't have what I needed, whether it was love, finances, shelter, necessities, or presence, and I'm thankful for that. As a teenager, though, I started to realize my struggle and experience with broken-heartedness from my father's absence began to play out in every platonic and romantic relationship I was in from then until recent years: it was not healthy. And I'm ready to share why.

Gem

THEY take over when YOU ignore the red flags.

Too Many Withdrawals and Not Enough Deposits

Friendships, Family, and Romantic Relationships were deeply tainted by my thought of needing to hold onto everyone. I was keeping people around me for all the wrong reasons. I don't regret anything I've done for anyone, but I regret my actions on the consistency of doing it even when they showed me I was being used. The word "used" makes my skin crawl, yet I still longed for people not to leave. So I started praying to God to understand how to free myself. I didn't realize it would come with an eye-opening reality and awareness of red flags that I constantly ignored.

Gem

Love Is Blind. Pay attention to how LOVE is showing up in your life.

Entry 5:

Love Doesn't Hurt

Love Doesn't Hurt

How many people can raise their hand and agree that they haven't experienced a healthy romantic relationship? You watch Love Jones, Poetic Justice, Jason Lyric, The Best Man, and couples reciting Ciara's prayer on social media. Yet, you still end up with the wrong person in a bad situation? How many can raise their hand and agree that they've ignored the yellow light, red light, or just a deer in front of headlights in romantic relationships? I scratched the surface of this topic in *A Better Me*, but I was too afraid to grab the shovel and dig a little deeper. Not anymore, though; I'm all in the mud trying to dig up trauma, dissect it, and create a clean foundation of lessons, healing, and growth that I didn't think was possible. I know what it feels like to be with someone who just wanted you for money, sex, arm candy, and an option. I know what it feels like to give a past partner chance after chance, even when the lies and deceit stared you in the face. I've even experienced emotional and verbal abuse in a relationship. And if I weren't in therapy at the time and a stage in my life of healing and rebirth, I would've ignored everything that transpired in the abusive relationship and done the ultimate no-no: STAY.

My closest friends and family have always come to me for advice because of the many unfortunate life happenings I've experienced. Yet, I hated that I could give sound advice to others in the past, but I didn't instill the advice within myself and my well-being until now. Sharing these past experiences will provide an understanding of how far I've come and what I am NOT willing to settle for in the present or the future. I'm inspired to tell the truth, the whole truth, and nothing but the truth.

Read On.

Gem

Look in the mirror, and ask yourself, "am I being truthful with myself."

Entry 6:
Truth Hurts

* * * * * * * * * * * * * *

Truth Hurts

S had was not the man for me. I should have left Shad when he cheated the first time.

There's no way I could have written or said that sentence years ago and believed it. But now, I'm willing to dig deep and better understand why I put up with mistreatment for so long. Shad and I met in our childhood neighborhood, Cabrini Green, on Chicago's Near North Side. Our Stanton Park gymnasium was everyone's safe haven in the community. Stanton Park was where we laughed, played, started friendships, had annual talent shows, cried together, and treasured our upbringing before social media and technology took over.

When I met Shad there, he stood out to me; he was nicely dressed, with good hygiene, confidence, and a smile everyone loved. I remember the first time he made me smile, on Valentine's Day, when we took our first picture together, intertwined in one another's arms, with our spray-painted shirts on. I remember everyone looked on with smiles, cheering us on, and throughout those years together, those same smiles from everyone turned into laughter and whispers.

"He cheating on that girl."

"She's so stupid."

"That boy is using her."

I heard those phrases from my closest friends, his friends, and associates. And I internally felt all of it yet chose to ignore it because I wanted him to notice that I always had his back, no matter what people said or did.

No Matter What!

In the present. No Matter What is NOT in my vocabulary because -No Matter What had turned into Shad's thinking, cheating was acceptable. And my staying with him throughout his serial infidelity made him even more comfortable doing it.

I learned that you must be cautious with certain things you say because sometimes people will take it for granted and twist it around to create their interpretation. And Shad took that phrase, No Matter What, and ran with it. Shad would continue to cheat, get caught, and then become creative with hiding it. I knew I didn't want a cheating man; I deserved better! But I was still there trying to fix him.

I remember when my son first started walking. I would stand behind him, trying to break his fall. I was nervous and didn't want him to stumble over anything. Now imagine me doing that to a grown man. I was standing behind Shad, trying to break his fall: obstacles, storms, unfortunate life happenings, emotional moments. Yet, every time I fell from his infidelity and lies, there was no one to break my fall, and each fall hurt worse than the previous one.

Shad was cheating on me when he passed away. The night he passed, I received a phone call from one of my former best friends with the side chick on the other line. Yes, you read it correctly; *one of my former best friends called me three-way with Shad's side chick on the other line.*

It went like this.

The cell phone vibrated. I was sitting in my bedroom with one of my soul sisters, Sah, who came quickly to see about me the night Shad passed away. A soul sister is a friend who becomes more like an extended sister due to the bond, connection, and years of friendship.

Seeing that one of my best friends was calling, I answered.

My Best Friend whispers through the phone:

"I wanted to reach back out to check on you, and I have someone else on the line who would like to send their condolences. "

Side Chick is crying: "Martina, this is Keisha; I wanted to confess that I've been romantically seeing Shad for a while. I know you are his woman. And I will not be at the funeral out of respect for you. My prayers are with you."

I can't make this up!

Keisha, the side chick who has a close bond with my former best friend, persuaded my best friend to call me 3 hours after Shad passed away to tell me this. At that moment, I was still trying to process everything. I had my phone on speaker so Sah could hear everything. Sah snatched my phone, exchanged curse words at my best friend and Keisha, then hung the phone up. To find out that Shad was cheating on me with someone I knew because she was close to my best friend had to be the most humiliating thing to experience in a time of grief.

Keisha knew Shad, and I was together. Everyone from our community knew. And my former best friend knew calling me was not cool, and my loyalty and trust for my best friend disappeared because of that phone call.

A week before Shad passed, Shad and I talked about how we were progressing in our relationship.

"No more cheating and lying, Martina; I'm all in, " he said. A week later, on the day of his passing, I was sitting on my bed, shaking, embarrassed, and angry, and I couldn't call the person who had once again hurt me.

"I am so stupid."

"I should have known better."

"Why did I stay after all these years of deceit."

I was taking jabs at myself for something someone else had done. As a result, I felt unpretty emotionally, mentally, and physically.

Shad's untimely death woke me up; I became aware of my "fix them" disease pattern:

Stick around longer.

Can I fix what he's doing?

Can I help him change? **Which turned into tearing my soul up.** I didn't know what to do to heal from my anger, so I continued to carry it inside with no outlet. I had distanced myself from my former best friend because of the side chick saga. My soul was in a constant danger zone filled with the paranoia of disloyalty and true colors from others. But let me tell you, holding your emotions hostage is never a good idea. Because when the feelings seep out, it is not in a healthy way. I knew it was time to get back to therapy.

I met my first trauma therapist, Mrs. Childs, during my first year in college. Trauma therapy helps heal parts of you that you do not care to relive, ones you would rather keep silent and hidden. Trauma therapy recognizes and emphasizes traumatic experiences starting from childhood.

My first therapy session with Mrs. Childs was eye-opening. But unfortunately, I went into the session already guarded because of my prior experience with therapy. However, Mrs. Childs immediately sensed my resistance and began asking me about my previous experience with treatment. What stood out in our first session was that Mrs. Childs was talking with me and not at me; she discussed her experience with not-so-great therapy and let me set the foundation for what I wanted to discuss.

Mrs.Childs created a safe and nonjudgemental environment for me to unpack my past. In addition, our conversation surrounding my relationship with Shad enhanced my understanding and awareness that the bond was unhealthy. And as my therapy sessions continued, I realized that I hadn't started the healing process and still hadn't forgiven him. The most impactful assignment Mrs. Childs gave me was to write a letter to Shad, go to his grave, and read the letter aloud.

The four-page letter I wrote him discussed my embarrassment, anger, and resentment. It broke down each affair that I was aware of that Shad had. It described how much it changed me for the worse. The letter expressed why I kept taking him back after calling it quits and shared why I should've stayed gone. I wrote that letter with tears falling and hitting the paper. I finished writing that letter crying myself to sleep.

I read the four-page letter to Shad at his gravesite on his death anniversary. I remember sitting on the leaves-filled ground in front of his tombstone, wailing the words out. I stared at the picture on his tombstone as the four-page letter ended. My last words on the page were: *I forgive you.*

I remember going silent, with the Sun beaming in my face, and I could hear the leaves crunching under my legs.

I returned to Mrs. Childs's office feeling like a different person the following week. She asked me if I could read the letter aloud to her. I read the four-page letter, shaking, wailing, with flashbacks of Shad scattering my thoughts.

After reading the last words on the page, I forgive you, Shad, I yelled out, and I forgive my former best friend too.

I couldn't believe the words that exited my mouth. I didn't even realize I was standing up while reading it. I wiped my face and slowly sat back down, with Mrs. Childs observing and smiling at me, uttering the words, "Martina, this is what you call a healing breakthrough."

I left Mrs. Childs's office with a better perspective. I credited therapy and the tools used throughout our sessions to my next breakthrough of ending a toxic relationship that I was in at the time of treatment because the connection was parallel to my relationship with Shad. Therapy with Mrs. Childs opened a pathway of forgiveness and awareness that I needed in my life.

Mrs. Child's mission was to help me become aware of the work I needed to continue, slowly peeling back the layers of pain while being gentle with myself. She was my therapist during my entire college career. Unfortunately, our sessions ended because she took her therapy practice back to her home state. Nevertheless, I was happy for her and appreciated the enlightening breakthroughs during our four years of sessions together.

After her departure and my graduation from college, I was determined to learn how to embed the tools, lessons, and exercises Mrs. Childs taught me in my everyday life. However, I struggled with staying the course and found myself going backward. Have you ever experienced picking at a wound that hasn't had a chance to heal fully and suddenly starts bleeding again? My painful past remained present because I kept doing that, picking, until it fully bled.

Gem

I want you to put this book down, stand in the mirror, and tell the person looking back, "I love you."

Now pick the book back up: we got more Gems to read.

The woman in the mirror

The woman in the mirror

As an adult, I've realized relationships from every walk of life can make or break you: relationships with your family, friends, teachers, children, managers, colleagues, business partners, and significant others. You can learn many things to push you forward or keep you on a path toward nowhere. Relationships shape you and teach you something about life, most notably yourself, that no one else can. But it's up to you to pay attention to what you are telling yourself, what you are keeping around, the things you emphasize more, and the people you are better off without.

I always tell people one of my favorite sermons is from Bishop TD Jakes.

"There are people who can walk away from you. And hear me when I tell you this! When people can walk away from you: let them walk. I don't want you to try to talk another person into staying with you, loving you, calling you, caring about you, coming to see you, staying attached to you. I mean, hang up the phone. When people can walk away from you, let them walk. Your destiny is never tied to anybody that left."

I started channeling Bishop TD. Jake's words and Mrs. Child's examples into daily affirmations I recited aloud, to myself, and by myself when looking in the bathroom mirror every morning. Affirmations are positive words and phrases that you can repeat daily to retrain your mind, body, and spirit for the better. The affirmations resonated, spoke volumes, and brought the terms "forgiveness" and "let it go" to the forefront of every aspect of my experiences. I began to feel a shift that caused me to let go and walk away from people and things that were no longer healthy for me. Of course, many didn't like the change, and I honestly didn't care because I spent too much time carrying baggage that needed to be dropped.

Gem

Let It, Them, Him GO.

Bag Lady

Bag Lady

"Let it go. Let it go. Let it go. Let it go." I listen to Erykah Badu's melody from her song Bag Lady and instantly relate to the many phrases and even the video visual interpretation of how the things you carry and hold on to can weigh you down emotionally, mentally, spiritually, physically, and financially. I was carrying mine and everyone else's bags until all the bags made me drop to my knees and cry out to God for help. I didn't want to be a fixer anymore, and I didn't want to continue to attract platonic and romantic relationships in my life that were only there to take and leave. So I was no longer interested in carrying other people's stuff. And that didn't sit well with others.

There's a huge bag I had been carrying for many years that I knew was about to burn.

Gem

When someone shows you who they are, **believe them the first time**."Maya Angelou"

Part 1: The death of my alter ego: Sponge

The death of my alter ego: Sponge

Sponges are used to wash dishes and absorb everything it comes into contact with; However, after repeatedly using the Sponge, it doesn't feel the same, nor does it look the same. Over time you have to replace the Sponge to go through the same process the last Sponge did. I hate to say that I was a sponge for many years for many people, especially financially.

I learned the value of working hard, saving, and owning my own early. My mother Elaine and my grandmother Rosie showed in their actions, work ethic, raising, and teachings how you can make a living and take care of your business and family. I instilled these teachings into my everyday life, and although it was a good thing for me to create a healthy financial journey, it became my downfall as a sponge to others.

I wanted everyone to feel good and be stress-free. So if someone asked me for anything, I ran to assist. Even if I was low on funds, I still gave my last. You would think this addiction kicked off in my adult years, but this started in my teenage years. And yes, I said an addiction because that's what it was, being addicted to being a sponge. Friends would ask me for money, funds to buy their food, or the favor of holding some cash while never paying it back.

My heart of gold is an excellent trait for good people and good causes. But, it was damaging me. The "heart of gold" and "fix it disease" was in a toxic zone that I didn't recognize. Yet years of therapy began to clarify my understanding of just how dangerous it was for my mental and finances. People flocked to me in a chameleon form showing just how ruthless one's motives are to someone with a good heart.

Part 2: Money Is The Root Of All Evil

Money Is The Root Of All Evil

A LARGE sum of money within a 3-month time frame is what I gave Max, a childhood friend with who I formed a one-sided romantic relationship. I know that was a mouth full to take in, and it worsens.

Since childhood, Max and I have connected through a mutual friend to whom he is related. He always liked me, yet I was in a relationship with Shad, so I kept it respectful and platonic. However, when Shad passed away, Max expressed how he felt about me, and during my healing time from Shad's passing, letting Max inside my heart was the biggest mistake I made.

MONEY!

I remember the first time Max asked me for some money. He told me that it was for the rent that he was behind in.

Old Martina tolerated any story without investigating the facts and immediately jumping to assist.

New Martina, examine every intricate detail before I am even willing to continue to listen.

I felt terrible for Max in the Old Martina days because he always struggled financially and was constantly in turmoil. Max faced timed me on my birthday, the same year he asked for help with his rent money after I had not heard from him since he called to ask for the favor and received the money. Looking back now, when he wished me a happy birthday, the conversation should've ended there. Yet, later that night, in a vulnerable state, I decided to invite him to my hotel room after my birthday gatherings with my close family and friends.

Bad Idea.

Intuition is important. Please don't do something when your soul tells you NOT to do it. Easier said than done; this is my lesson on that.

Max arrived at the wrong hotel down the street from my hotel. God's plan was to stop him from even coming to my hotel.

Old Martina stubbornly had difficulty listening to GOD and INTUITION.

New Martina doesn't have that problem after extended, intense meditation, spiritual, and therapy practices.

MONEY!

Max called to advise me that he was at the wrong hotel and had no money to get to my hotel. So I sent him a rideshare car to my hotel. He arrived; we went upstairs and started having a conversation. And unfortunately, I was intoxicated from the celebration with my family and friends earlier, which didn't make that moment of vulnerability and sexual arousal any better.

We had sex, and it was terrible.

I am a monogamous, serious relationship, praying for a marriage type of woman. Once I'm with someone, I devote my time, energy, love, and intimacy to them and only to them. However, that moment with Max felt different, and I wouldn't say I liked him or myself that day. Max fell asleep instantly, and I lay there saying this would never happen again.

MONEY!

The following day, I paid for another rideshare for him to get back to his place, and we went our separate ways.

But that wasn't it.

MONEY!

Christmas time was approaching. Max called to tell me he couldn't afford to get Christmas presents for his two kids and stepchild. I have a soft spot for kids, but their parents, though? Old Martina: does.

New Martina: investigate everything.

Old Martina gave Max a lot of money to get his kids something for Christmas. He said thank you, and I heard back from him in the new year.

Max had a habit of calling me around the 1st of the month when rent was due, or I would typically send a text to say hi, and then the begging would start. Max thought he nailed manipulation and found his next victim because he had a track record of being a womanizer. He had no clue I was on the cusp of my reset.

I decided to address with my new trauma therapist, Mrs. Rose, the back and forth I had with Max for three months and how it made me feel.

I had to take that transparency walk of shame with my therapist, who started me on a practice called: NO. I had to say no to anything that didn't serve a purpose or didn't reciprocate. Max didn't like my new word. Due to this, Max blocked me on social media. So I reached out to him through FaceTime to ask what his issue was; he appeared annoyed on FaceTime, and his words were distant and cold. This was the Max that our mutual friend had warned me about; this was the Max that his own family warned me about; after that, Max blocked me via phone, and I never heard from him again. I found out he was in a toxic relationship at the time and was using me. The word "used" was charred that day, and the Sponge died.

Gem

Change can be uncomfortable, but if it's for the better good: it's worth it.

Entry 10:
Face-Off

Face-Off

Nipsey Hussle said a quote in one of his songs that states, "But what is a mistake without the lesson? See, the best teacher in life is your own experience. None of us know who we are until we fail" Everything that I have been through and still conquering was rushing through my mind, body, and soul. I shared with my therapist this, and we started a treatment plan for Reset Boot Camp. It was time to write down everything still bleeding in me. I won't go in-depth into my reset process with my therapist because it's truly personal and sacred for me, but I will share some highlights and gems in the following entries. Read On.

Gem

Whenever you are headed to a different destination and level, you will have to Let Go, Forgive People and Things that will hinder your next step.

Single Mother

Single Mother

Iam a Single Mother. I have been a Single Mother for eight years. Everyone is constantly shocked to find out that I am as if it's poisonous to be a single mother. However, there are many single mothers around the world:

By choice (their wishes or medical procedures to have a child/ children),

By force (due to the death of the father, addiction of the father, or imprisonment of the father),

By life lessons (having a child with someone who is not ready or understands the importance of being responsible for another human being), and then there are

The unfortunate ones (because of absent dads for excuses we will constantly be trying to comprehend for years).

My situation falls into the category of Life Lessons. Since I was a child, the guidance I learned from my mother and how she handled Justice was that she never degraded him or shared intricate details with others outside her safe circle. My sisters and I also developed our interpretation and understanding of our father because of what WE went through.

And because of that wise example- I hold that same sacred respect for my child's father. Therefore, I will not go in-depth about the journey with my child's father. Still, I am willing to talk about my emotions, reawakening moments, struggles through my eyes, being a single parent, and how I worked on forgiving my son's father so that I can be internally healthy & whole for my son.

One thing I've noticed is that many women are angry at the father of their children, which takes away from their kids being able to see their mother whole and present (emotionally, physically, and mentally for them). So many kids get the anger that is supposed to be for the absent parent taken out on them, which is not cool.

I knew I would be a single parent the day I delivered my son. My son's father decided he didn't love me anymore and wished we would've waited to have a child. I tried so hard to get him to change his mind but couldn't. So instead, I learned that I had a child with someone who was the replica of my father. Seeing the pattern sent me into the emotional turmoil of begging my child's father to be present so my child wouldn't experience his father's absence like I experienced growing up.

Read my following words carefully.

You cannot force someone to be a father.

I repeat: you cannot force someone to be a father.

Being a father is something they need to learn on their own with positive support, reality slaps, good people in their lives holding them accountable, positive examples, and GOD guiding them. That affirmation and understanding you just read above are what I live by; within my journey of acceptance and forgiveness.

It was hard, though; I was literally on bending knees for my son's father to be present. Yet, my knees continue to bleed, trying to force it to happen. So through prayer and therapy, I finally learned how to stop, and losing it all made me wake up.

My testimony at a specific time frame in my life was the following: I was on my last dollar, lost my beautiful home, and had nowhere to go, and I called my child's father for help- his words: "I ain't got it. I don't know what to tell you."

When I heard those words, it burned my soul because I had never asked him for anything. I worked hard for anything my son needed, and when my health knocked on death's door, I, unfortunately, lost it all. And all he could say was: I don't have it.

My son's father slandered me all over social media during that time. He disrespected my family, who showed him sympathy and empathy and created false narratives about me, causing me to reach my breaking point.

I remember sitting in a session with my therapist Mrs. Rose and wailed all of this out to her. She stared; her facial expression turned into my mother's being fed up. Finally, Mrs. Rose said: "we will end the pattern of dating, dealing with, and letting in the replica of your father: TODAY. "

I underwent a 6-month treatment with Mrs. Rose of tears, lots of shedding flaws, and lots of hidden strength. I thank Mrs. Rose, my mother, and GOD for getting me through that process of turning the hatred I had built in my heart for my son's father into forgiveness towards him for my emotional, mental, physical, and spiritual being. Then, finally, I took my POWER back.

Single Mothers, work on your healing for your babies.

Single Mothers, work on life and purpose for your babies.

Single Mothers, let your babies see you for YOU: happy, healthy, and ready to show them what a bounce-back represents.

I watch a lot of women on Social Media entertaining their kid's father's dysfunction, sharing their business with people who don't even care about them; those people are just glued to their phones, laughing.

In 8 years, my son has only seen me ONCE break down, which was the moment I described earlier of losing it all. And I vowed for him not to ever see me like that again. And by God's Grace, he has not.

Social Media has never seen me slander and gossip about my son's father because I know better- my mother's life with Justice taught me to gain my POWER back, live in my truth, and GOD will handle the rest.

And in the present, GOD is taking care of it.

Single Moms, I want to leave you with this. Treat your babies right, with unconditional love. They did not ask to be here; YOU brought them into this world. YOU. Give them the upbringing of healthy, happiness, unconditional love, safety, selflessness, and being taken care of- they deserve it.

Entry 12:

Daddy, I need you!

Daddy, I need you!

I remember going from being in a hospital bed, told I almost died, to being homeless.

I remember I had to take medical leave from work, which reduced my earnings.

I remember after my health insurance took its portion out, I exhausted all my savings to pay for my portion of the medical bills and continue to provide for my son.

I remember the day, and I remember the year my mother was residing with me to help aid in the care of my son while I battled with my health crisis. I remember the day we had to fill up our cars and a Uhaul truck with my possessions.

I remember my mother saying, " I will call Justice."

I had never heard my mother say that, and she was in tears. I hadn't lived in the same household as Justice since I was 11. I stared at her and told her to call him.

At that moment, my soul died.

She went to her car, sat there, and I could see her tears fall. I looked at my son in the back seat of my car in his car seat, having no understanding of what was taking place. He was so tiny at the time, and I was relieved that he was because, in the present, he has no recollection of it.

My mother rolled down her window and said, "he said come on." And we drove to Justice's house, trialing one another. I was in so much pain, still recovering from my health decline, boiling about my son's father's remark, "I don't know what to tell you," and feeling like I had failed as a woman, daughter, and mother.

We spent four months at Justice's house, which was HELL. When I needed Justice the most, he was not there emotionally, physically, or mentally, regardless of him letting us come there; we were not welcomed. Overhearing his phone conversations with others, I remember everyone telling him that he should not have allowed us to come there and that we should go to a homeless shelter. I remember walking in from work one evening and hearing him having that conversation, and it tore my heart up. Yet, it gave me the strength to create my bounce back sooner than later.

I remember calling my manager, Joc, with whom I had a brother and sister bond, and told him I had to return to work earlier than expected.

Joc said, "Martina, you know you are not well enough."

I responded, Joc, let me explain.

I opened up to Joc about my upbringing and what I was facing at that moment. You could hear his whimpers through the phone.

Joc responded, "Martina, you have to get out of there; come back to work, but you have to promise me that you will take it easy."

I went back to work full-time, attending all my physical therapy appointments, trauma therapy appointments, and doctor visits. I was tired but had to get out of Justice's house. That year, a week before my birthday and four months into physical recovery, I got approved for my new place. My place was out of sight, out of mind by GOD's grace. I was thankful, humble, and appreciative of the power of prayer and hard work. We were settled in our new home on Christmas Eve that year.

I was ecstatic; I was physically getting my strength back, excelling at work, and working on my emotional, physical, and mental health. But I began to notice the hatred built in my heart again towards Justice, and everything I had experienced as a child with him returned to the surface, causing my trauma therapist, Mrs. Rose to place me on another complex therapy treatment to heal, accept, and forgive Justice.

The treatment was brutal-having to reveal dirty laundry and realize just how bad the internal wounds were. Yet, I was relieved once I began seeing and feeling the treatment process working for me. Some people spend their entire lives hating the absent parent. And as the saying goes:you end up marrying your father, and I didn't want that for myself, my son, and our future. That intense therapy with Mrs. Rose helped me understand and avoid that from happening, especially in the following situation I'm willing to be transparent about- I have to dedicate this next section to survivors of abuse and the ones we have lost: physically, emotionally, and verbally. Here's my story.

Gem

The POWER of Purple is taking YOUR power back.

Purple Ribbons. Purple Flowers. I am a Domestic Violence Survivor.

Purple Ribbons. Purple Flowers. I am a Domestic Violence Survivor.

I am a domestic violence survivor. I say that with faith and motivation. Very few people close to me are aware of this story, yet I'm willing to share it because I want my beautiful people out there to understand that:

Love doesn't hurt.

Love doesn't manipulate.

Love doesn't lie.

Love doesn't hit.

Love doesn't cheat.

Love doesn't bleed.

Love doesn't disrespect.

None of the above: Is Love.

Leave the person who hit you.

Leave the person who threatens you.

Leave the person who slanders your name and calls you names.

Leave the person who cheats on you.

Leave the person who belittles you.

Leave for YOU.

DO NOT meet with them one last time.

Please do not accept any gifts from them.

Block Them from having contact with you.

Look into domestic violence programs, go to the police, call a lawyer, and tell someone you love, who truly cares, what's going on. And please remember, when getting to know someone or even if you knew them already: Gather information from your mate's past to learn more about them, especially their previous relationships. If they are hesitant about providing information or examples about their previous relationships- red flag; pay attention to it. If you need to take the additional step of doing a background check on them-DO IT, don't hesitate to do such. You are protecting YOU.

Beautiful People understand that there is sunshine after the storm. Beautiful People understand you should never settle just because you're comfortable with religious matters, family dynamics, or think no one else would want you.

Purple Ribbons and Purple Flowers. RESET YOUR POWER.

I met Rick on a dating site. When you are a constant, busy person, there's little time to meet anyone like many of us did back in the day (through childhood, school, and upbringing). The two previous serious relationships I've been in were with people I knew for a long time. Yet, my plate was getting busier, and I decided to take a chance at a dating site.

Rick's profile stood out to me when I noticed his "like" to get my attention; his profile reflected a similar interest in writing, positivity, and no thirst trap pics (grey jogging pants). So I reached out to him via a message to inquire more about his passion for writing. We messaged back and forth about interests, likes, and dislikes then he provided me with his number. I informed him that we would set up a FaceTime vibe check because I wanted to ensure it was him and not a catfish.

The following day we FaceTime, and it was him. A lovely, well-groomed gentleman who answered more of my questions with a sense of compassion. Rick and I communicated via text daily and set up a FaceTime vibe when our schedules permitted, which was our routine for two months, getting to know one another before I decided to meet him in person.

Our chemistry was spot-on; we conversed more during our first in-person meeting and had a lovely time. But that was the end of the excellent time, and here's why.

First, I researched Rick to understand better who he is and came across his social media page. I read a caption that stated: **I did almost a 10-year bid, but I survived.**

10-year bid. I was very privy to what a "bid" meant: **prison**. I sat numb. But I insisted on knowing more about this bid, so I searched more. The information I came across changed the game: Rick had multiple mug shots and was the headline, years back, in the news for a crime. I will not reveal further information out of respect for his privacy regarding that incident.

I felt misled and deceived; one of the first questions I had asked him two months prior was to tell me about his previous relationships and anything about his past that he thought I should know. Instead, the picture Rick painted of himself as someone applying for a job with a Resume filled with lies. I contacted him about the information I found, and he flipped out.

"You were snooping," he said.

"I didn't think I had to share that; it's my past; it doesn't affect you," he said.

And the different excuses he provided multiplied with his tone and conversation going into a Jekyll and Hyde effect for months.

What we had should have ended there, but Old Martina was trying to take over; the fix-it disease was trying to wake up in me. And I kept silent about it from my family, therapist, and close friends.

UNTIL...

He became verbally and emotionally abusive toward me. He begged me for sex that I refused to give. Rick called my phone at all times of the night, accused me of cheating, and said that if I received messages on social media from random people, it was just people hating him. Rick created fake social media pages to degrade me, create lies, and write fake reviews about my books online.

I knew I had to end it and get the cops involved when we were in a hotel room at 1 in the morning after a night on the town, and he stood in my face, hovering over me as if he was about to swing after yelling and asking who was on my phone.

"Get out of my face Rick," I said, glancing over at the lamp on a nearby table to pick up.

Rick moved closer.

I sat holding my phone, with my father's number to press, and I couldn't. I just froze and crumbled inside; because, at that moment: I needed my father.

I glanced up at Rick with my hand on the lamp.

"take two steps back, or I will bust you in the face," I yelled.

He was surprised to receive my response. Instead, he stepped back, fell onto the bed in the room, and fell asleep. I sat up all night with the lamp in my hand. As soon as the sun rose, I hopped in the shower and quickly left.

Rick continued to taunt me on social media for months as my legal team began making sure I was good and safe. Finally, I had to sit with my mother and be transparent about the entire ordeal. I told my trauma therapist, Mrs. Rose, what transpired within those months, and she placed me on another treatment plan to process what had happened. After that, I went on Hiatus for a while to heal. Hurt People, Hurt People.

I learned a lot about myself. If I had let Old Martina fully take over, I would have stayed, trying to make things better for him: yet I realized he was a broken man with more hidden secrets being revealed as time passed.

New Martina regained her power, knowing I needed to safely remove myself from this situation because I knew how domestic violence could transpire and end. Purple Ribbons. Purple Flowers, I am a domestic violence survivor.

Gems

God hears your silent cries, yet don't be afraid to yell them out to him.

The Reset

Entry 14-Entry 20: The Reset

Reset Therapeutic Bootcamp was the haven I didn't know I needed. It taught me so much about myself and life. It made me put the sole focus and investment in my healing and transformation with a circle of excellent professional trauma therapists.

In the following sections, I want to share some moments throughout my Reset Bootcamp diary entries I believe can provide Gems to you in your healing journey. We'll start with the Seven Pillars of Healing.

Seven Pillars Of Healing

Pillar One: Nutritional Balancing

What do you eat, and how can you increase your nutritional intake? What kind of water are you drinking, and how much?

I increased my water intake and decreased my intake of fruity drinks for more natural smoothies.

Pillar Two: Emotional Health

What brings joy to your heart? How do you hold your emotional stress in your body?

The joys of my heart are my son, family, close friends, and my passion for writing and inspiring. Which helps balance out my peace and happiness. My emotional stress covered my entire body, stopping all daily functions in the past. In the present, emotional stress is felt in my head and behind my ears which is when I incorporate progressive EFT to calm me.

Pillar Three: Body-Mind Integration

Progressive EFT is a healing exercise to rid the body of negative emotions and toxic energy. The activity requires no equipment, no giant space, and no difficulties; it works wonders on the mind, body, and soul. I use it daily to help me navigate throughout my day.

Progressive EFT, the exercise is known as tapping -- and it is what it sounds like-tapping. To do it, begin by turning your hands palm-side up and gently tap the sides of your hands, chest points, chin, nose, and temple.

Pillar Four: Lifestyle Coaching

Trauma Therapy with a professional. I've been in therapy for over 18 years (6 of those years solely focused on trauma therapy) and am a walking testimony to it working. Like romantic and platonic relationships, you must investigate, connect, and find the therapist that best fits your needs and wants. Unfortunately, seeing a therapist is looked down upon in the Black and Brown communities because no one speaks about it and is scared to admit that they are in therapy.

Beautiful People, I'm going to be transparent with you—so many of you holding and reading this book in your hand need therapy. You are dealing with childhood traumas and cycles of brokenness and generational curses that you need to shed light on and be open to help. So many free therapy services are available for your exposure. But only YOU are standing in your way, so get out of your way, do the work, and start the healing path.

Pillar Five: Exercise Routine

What exercise suits you best?

My favorites are meditation-breathing techniques that help you align and silence your mind. And yoga- is a more spiritual exercise focusing on bringing harmony between mind, body, and soul. I've been doing both for 18 years, which has changed my mental and physical state.

Pillar Six: Living Environment

How do your peace and sanity align in your home? First, make sure you are not allowing the spirits of others into your home that do not serve the purpose of relaxation, well-being, safety, and happiness.

Pillar Seven: Soul Connection

Your soul knows what you came here to do. It knows your destiny and how to fulfill it in the most graceful and fulfilling way. But unfortunately, sometimes we lose connection with it, or the pain in our lives disconnects us, which is when meditation comes into play.

Seven Pillars of Forgiveness: My Candid Experiences

Pillar One: Understanding (Reconnecting with one of my childhood best friends during a storm in their life)

One of my childhood male best friends suffered an untimely tragic loss. I spoke to him occasionally throughout the years, but not as often as I did in the past. Our bond hit a rough patch years ago, and I will not go into what caused that rough patch, yet I will say that at that moment of tragic loss in his life, none of that past stuff mattered to me. In those moments is when the importance of forgiveness and understanding displays itself. And when the people I love need me, regardless of how many years it's been-I'm there.

When he called me to inform me that his mom had been in the hospital, I did not waste any time making my way to him to spend the entire day with him and his mother. But unfortunately, she passed a few months later, and I knew I had to continue to be there with constant contact and check-ins with him ever since. An essential trait I learned by doing that is " the importance of understanding" because you can humble yourself and learn and heal from others with love.

Pillar Two: Freedom (Getting Your Power Back)

We touched on this a little earlier in the book about how I reached out to Justice and my son's father during a difficult time in my life. They had complete power over me for years- the power of my emotional dysfunction. Not anymore. Getting My Power Back took a lot of trauma therapy sessions with my therapist Mrs. Rose to cleanse what was hurting me.

I learned: don't blame myself for what someone else did. And that, there, for me, was my turning point. You forgive for YOU, not the other person. Remember that.

Pillar Three: Remedy (Being transparent about how you are feeling).

I had a problem hiding my feelings from everybody until I burst emotionally. I learned the proper tools for expressing myself through transparency, and now I don't hold anything back. Understanding the level of openness with self and others took time, and still taking time. But the feeling I get on the inside, of pure clarity and wholeness, makes me appreciate my honesty with others in the present.

Pillar Four: Warmth (being gentle with self)

Being gentle with myself was tough for me. I always was hard on myself. So I began a mindful exercise that would redirect what I would say to myself in the moment of negativity and turn it into positivity.

Anything I would say negatively to myself or about myself, I would cut myself off and say aloud: "would you say this to your son?" three breaths in. three breaths out.

So I would hold that last breath and then hold my chest with a full exhale. It took me about six months to master-and. I'm still mastering it, as you read.

Pillar Five: Enhancement (honoring your progress)

Giving yourself flowers is genuinely needed. Every day, I take out a notebook and thank myself for each milestone I've taken on the path of internal healing. I also have talks aloud with GOD to honor how I'm feeling at that moment alongside side goals I have in mind. Finally, I close it out with my son's favorite prayer line: In Jesus' Name. Amen.

Pillar Six: Hope (looking forward to your healing for years to come).

This one is a big one. Think about a mental vision board for your healing process. I started this one three years ago, and each year I see myself conquering something through healing that I didn't think was possible.

Pillar Seven: Continuance (don't stop the process, continue to achieve internal recovery).

Every day is a new day to continue adding to internal healing. It is no secret that I've been through A LOT. But where I was and where I am now, I credit my constant focus on internal healing, gratitude, and peace.

Gems

Stop Just Existing. And Start Living.

Healing Is Here

Healing Is Here

Hiatus is my mind, body, and soul getaway, where I put everything on pause. It's a journey that I embark on annually to reset. Where I invest in the healing process. Let's be honest; cleansing your mindset, healing your spirit, and embracing change are complex, but working to come out better is worth it.

During my last Hiatus journey, one of my goals was to come out truly loving myself.

It was important to start accepting happiness, love, and healthy blessings in my life for the present and going forward. So below are the three areas I worked on:

Mental Health: Still working with my trauma therapist, Mrs. Rose, during this journey, and I'm forever grateful for her patience, her transparency, and her non-judgment in walking with me through my healing journey.

Physical Health: Still a work in progress; I have so many health ailments that I'm battling at once. We will discuss my mental and emotional journey with my physical health in a later read.

Emotional Health: There's a difference between mental health and emotional health. Mental Health focuses solely on the mind and the brain, including hormonal balance. In contrast, emotional health focuses on coping with and managing emotions. Meditation, therapy, and affirmations discussed in earlier reads are a few processes I continue to use throughout my mental and emotional health journey.

After the Hiatus process, we discussed: Once complete, I was more open to self-love and happiness. The center of my being felt pure and honest, which was able to be in tune with each step of understanding, accepting, and wanting to feel better about me. The process is complex; you must be willing to do the work. It's not an overnight fix, and you may feel unpretty while amid things, but knowing as you conquer the journey, you will begin to see a difference in who you are and how you show up for yourself.

One Heart. One Life. One Voice.

One Heart. One Life. One Voice.

For years, my health has been my giant storm and is very personal for me, my family, and my close friends, so I will not discuss my health ailments. Instead, I'm willing to discuss my emotional and mental journey. I survived three PAST suicide attempts: the aftermath led to an impactful transformation internally, mentally, emotionally, and spiritually. Coming out of a mind, body, and soul storm while having the support of my family, close friends, and circle of trauma therapists helped me become a walking testimony. My testimony became: conquering life and accepting that my health ailments will be with me forever but will not define me. Instead of fighting my conditions, I joined forces with them, which helped me have power over my health ailments and not my conditions having control over me. This motivation created an inspirational mission for me to inspire hurting hearts never to give up.

One Heart: A Meditation Exercise

Hold the center of your chest.

Repeat this affirmation: I give myself permission to live my life.

Inhale & Exhale

Hold the center of your chest.

Repeat this affirmation: I give myself permission to love myself.

Inhale & Exhale

Hold the center of your chest.

Repeat this affirmation: I love myself.

Inhale & Exhale

Hold the center of your chest.

Repeat this affirmation: I love myself, I trust myself, I will be myself, and I have one heart.

Inhale & Exhale

Breathe...

I watched an MTV episode of Teen Mom Family Reunion where the women of the Teen Mom Franchise worked with Life Coach Cheyenne

Bryant. Cheyenne provided different affirmations throughout their sessions that could help guide them through their healing journey. Those affirmation examples are the ones I shared above that I incorporated into my daily affirmations and meditation routine.

I came up with One Heart because we only have one heart. The beautiful piece of our lifeline holds the weight of how we feel, breathe, and live.

One Life :

You have to start living and stop just existing. I've just started to live and embrace the beauty of life. When my health ailments had power over me, they prevented me from living a life I love. But, once I joined forces with my health ailments and formed a healthy understanding, I started living; this is still a work in progress because, let's face it, having any health ailment sucks and can sometimes pause your life when your body shuts down. Yet, in those moments, I learned to do something special for myself—such as a manicure & pedicure. I also visit my favorite ice cream parlor or coffee shop or blast some of my favorite old skool and 90s music, Isley Brothers, Monica, Keith Sweat, Joe, Tank, and TLC. Having those moments for myself helps my mental and emotional health when dealing with life's challenging moments with my health ailments.

One Voice: For years, I was always the silent one in the room, observing everything and everyone. I only spoke when I had something to say or present to give a speech. My voice is also only felt through words. So when people hear me speak in the present, they are amazed at how intellectual and transparent I am.

Life Challenges silenced my voice. I grew silent over the years due to being in situations where what I said was ignored, and my opinion belittled, or in childhood trauma with Justice where if I spoke-the unthinkable could happen. I was quiet for a while because of all of this. Then therapy changed the game for me.

Mrs. Rose challenged me to write a song for myself, documenting my pain, and she wanted me to read it aloud to her at the next session; I stared at her during our session as if she had farted in the room when she challenged me to this. I was up for the challenge but was afraid to sing it aloud.

I remember turning on Mary J Blige, My Life, closing my eyes, and writing my life pains in a song. It took me all of 30 minutes to pen my pain. Then, I found an instrumental version of Mary J Blige's music and sang my song aloud in the mirror. The words created flashbacks in my mind, and tears began to fall, but I kept singing. At that moment is when I knew I had gotten my voice back.

In my next session with Mrs. Rose, I sang, wailed, and rocked back and forth, watching her smile as I sang every word. My voice and tone were firm, and my chest relaxed. I kept singing and singing and signing; when I was done, Mrs. Rose said, "Martina, you got your voice back." And since that session, I have not let my voice go silent.

Entry 23:

The Return Of An Ex

The Return Of An Ex

The ex: Tim. You will have to revert to my first book, A Better Me, to get the story behind our relationship's demise. In the present, Tim reached out to me via social media with a four-page inbox asking me why did I leave him over ten years ago. I thought this had to be a prank because I remembered every detail of the lie, deceit, cheating, and painful rollercoaster of being in a relationship with Tim.

Then I thought this was God's way of letting me get the closure I needed while already being healed from the relationship's demise. There's no way Old Martina could have responded to Tim. Yet, New Martina was ready to let him know the piece of turd he was to me ten years ago. So I penned the message out and left no words or thoughts hidden. And I waited for his response. His first response read: "Martina, I'm sorry." Then, I saw the dotted lines appear, so I knew he was writing the rest of his response. While waiting for his answer, I went to his page and found out he was now married.

After looking through his page, I noticed he had sent another four-page message back. I couldn't believe what I had read next.

"do you still want me"?

I told him I was not and would never be interested in a married man or my painful past. God Bless you and your wife, and I ended the conversation at that. It doesn't matter how many years have passed; I may have grown and healed, but some people, like Tim, remain the same, and the best thing you can do is leave them in the past.

The End Of One Road. The Beginning Of A New One.

The End Of One Road. The Beginning Of A New One.

Some years back, when I lost everything, I found out who my real Framily (Friends and Family) were. During that time, I had people looking at me like I was less than them, as if all the times I've held them down, mentally, emotionally, and financially, disappeared from their memory bank. In addition, a few former friends I borrowed money from during that time were hounding me like bill collectors for payback. So I paid those few people back and left them entirely alone- I wanted nothing to do with them.

I always heard and read the sayings, phrases, quotes, and biblical scriptures, and even famous people who lost it all say, "they found out who was REAL during the darkest moments." I had promised myself not to let those people stop me from being who I am and having the heart I have towards those who genuinely care and have my back. So it was the end of the road for our friendship. But the beginning of a new one with the REAL ones.

You DESERVE to be here: Love Letter To Hurting Hearts

You DESERVE to be here. Love Letter To Hurting Hearts.

Hey You. Yes, You.

The one who is sitting in the car crying.

The one who is sitting in the bathroom crying.

The one who is sitting in the hospital crying.

The one who is overworking themselves to hide the pain.

The one on social media wearing the facade that everything is alright.

Please read the following words: It's okay NOT to be okay.

Hey You. Yes, You.

I want you to close your eyes and think about the moment in your life when you were happy. The moment of your life that brought you joy. Maybe it's a friend, significant other, a special place, a remarkable thing, your child/children, a family member, and even unique words. Keep thinking about it until you can visualize that moment, special place, or person. And hold that moment in your heart.

Hey You. Yes, You.

Stop hiding your scars, cuts, bruises, and brokenness. Instead, sit down and research therapy, talk with someone you trust who shows no judgment, and get on the path of internal healing. You are not alone. Someone out there can be the listening ear and shoulder you can lean on.

Hey You. Yes, You.

Don't write that "last pen or goodbye message on social media" Hey, people that see that message, don't comment on it; call them and get to them. They don't need words at that moment; they need love, no judgment, and your physical presence.

Hold on, Beautiful; Please Hold On.

Put the knife down.

Put the gun down.

Get out of that car.

Get off of that bridge.

Get out of that water.

Get off that window ledge.

You deserve to be here. You deserve to live.

I've been where you are and made a complete transformation and redemption. Beautiful, you can, and you will too.

You deserve to be here. You deserve to live.

Manifestation of Love, Success, and Happiness

Manifestation of Love, Success, and Happiness

Love: A few years back, I gave up on ever having and experiencing true love. I said it would be my child and me forever, and I was okay because I didn't want to deal with heartbreak again. However, through my internal healing and forgiveness journey alongside trauma therapy, my heart shifted from thinking this way because I deserved love, healthy love, and wanted to be loved.

I no longer wanted my past to deter me from what I truly felt I deserved. So I asked Mrs. Rose how I could set out on the path to be ready for true love when it comes, and we started a 6-month treatment process to engage and enter a new journey. During my treatment, I learned: that to be prepared for healthy love, you have to be willing to unpack the painful definition of what love is not from your past experiences to forgive and open your heart to what love should be.

I'm willing to share a specific part of my treatment that placed my heart in a position to be open to love again: Forgiveness Burn Letters. The forgiveness letters I wrote to each of my previous partners that I read aloud to Mrs. Rose and burned to remove the power of the past gave me the foundation to cleanse my view on love. Honestly, I WAS STILL HURTING when I wrote the forgiveness letter years back to Shad during my visit to the cemetery. However, the forgiveness letter I wrote recently to Shad was filled with more empathy, understanding, and evolution. The other letters to my exes followed the same pattern. I knew I had transitioned to a place in healing where I could be free of the hurt and more aware of the lesson.

Success: I've spent many years assisting others with their dreams, goals, and success and putting my projects and passions in the vault. At the time, I didn't even pay attention to what I was doing, putting myself last. In the present, I've paused all willing to help others unless they are dear to me and have been influential in my goals and accomplishments.

Embarking on this journey of self-focus, I have had to remove myself from different circles, connections, people, and things. And I'm okay with that because I call this time in my life Self Love. Self Focus. Self Success. And I realized that when you are focused on moving to new levels, new purposes, and different places in your life, everybody can't go.

You will also begin to see just how supportive people are. I began to wean out people who didn't want to see me prosper in my light. And that, for me, is a massive problem because I spent years being the cheerleader to others and holding the flashing light to support their shine. When I decided it was time to put myself first again, a lot of chatter started:

"How are you gonna be able to take care of this stuff for me."

"So you are saying you will focus on your craft."

I couldn't believe what people were asking me, yet I knew I was passionate about rebranding, revising, refocusing, and resetting. It was time to shine MY light again.

Happiness: The happiness you long for starts within you; the key to your happiness cannot be found in others; this is when internal healing is critical for anyone because so many people walk around acting as if they're happy but go home at night and completely break down. I know, that was the Old Martina.

MY HEART AND UNDERSTANDING OF MYSELF CHANGED when I started doing the internal work and unpacking the pain, fears, and failures. I was no longer willing to be unhappy. And to reduce the unhappiness, I had to make drastic changes to my emotional & mental health, spirituality, surroundings, people, places, and things.

I'm on my happiness journey, where my peace and mental health are paramount. Meditation is pivotal during this time because it helps me connect to what is lacking, what needs to be removed, and what to welcome in. This stage in my healing process is fragile because when you're getting ready to complete a 360 turn, lessons from different angles in your life (good and bad) will hit. For example, imagine yourself riding through a terrible rainstorm, holding on to the steering wheel, trying to remain calm, and focusing on the road. Suddenly the sun starts to appear, and the rain stops. That's a 360 moment.

Where am I now with Grief?

Where am I now with Grief?

The loss of my Granny Rosie and Shad was a few of the moments my heart stopped. Yet, I would not have healthily conquered grief without therapy during these devastating moments. Therapy is important. I have discussed this throughout the entire read. Back in the day, it was always said: what happens in the house stays in the house. And I'm so thankful my grandmother and mother went against that saying because it motivated me to seek help.

Granny Rosie

I discussed the passing of Granny Rosie in A Better Me. My grandmother is the Matriarch of The Common Family and played a massive role in my upbringing. It was no secret that I was Granny's Spoil Brat, eating mangoes and bacon bits with Granny Rosie, taking trips to Lincoln Park Zoo to collect sour apples, or assisting granny with her candy shop (best known for her ice cream). Unfortunately, when she passed, I fell into a deep depression. And during those times, my journal writing helped me. I would write journal entries to my grandmother titled: Hello To Heaven, letting her know how I was doing, my anger, and my frustration. I read each letter every night as I said my prayers for bed.

As an adult, I was still hurting from Granny Rosie's passing. My therapist Mrs. Rose developed a Grief Treatment process to unpack how I've been feeling for over 25 years since my granny's passing. The Grief Treatment has been packed with healing, understanding, coping skills, and ways to conquer grief healthily. A few coping skills are:

Express the pain

Don't hide how you are feeling. It is okay NOT to be okay, especially when you have lost someone dear to you.

Grief can trigger many different emotions.

You can be happy one minute, then angry, mad, and lashing out the next. You need a support system that understands and holds you up during these moments.

Everyone's grief looks different.

Do not compare your grief process to the following persons; everyone handles grief differently.

Seek out face-to-face support from a therapist.

Therapy does help with your grief process. I honestly would not be healthily handling grief today if it wasn't for my showing up to treatment to understand how to conquer distress and understand suffering.

Shad

My first book, A Better Me, discussed Shad's passing. He was my first love, and his murder took a toll on me emotionally, mentally, spiritually, and physically. My health declined, and I didn't see any return point to happiness. I was grieving losing him, my self-love, and the embarrassment of his infidelity all at the same time. Therapy helped me sort out my anger, emotions, grief, and lack of forgiveness. However, I learned in treatment that I couldn't grieve properly because I still hadn't forgiven him. I had to learn how to forgive someone no longer here on earth, which was not an easy task. The following technique is what I used to assist me on the forgiveness journey:

Writing a letter

I sat alone, visualized Shad, and wrote a pain-stricken letter detailing things I had left out in the first one I had written years ago. I didn't hold anything back, and I read it aloud alone. I was expecting to have tears falling and wailing like I did when I read the first one at the cemetery, but this time was different. I had this calming peace come over me that I had never experienced before, and in my next session with Mrs. Rose, I brought it up. She informed me that I had entered into a stage of acknowledgment and acceptance in my journey of forgiveness and grief. From that day forward, I started writing in a journal to Shad, explaining each moment of confusion and pain, detailing every embarrassment and my faults. I wasn't just forgiving him; I was forgiving myself, which set the path for a healthier self-love and grief journey.

Grief doesn't go away; you learn how to conquer & heal through it with different strategies, healthier coping techniques, and REAL loved ones & friends' support.

It would be best if you were not hard on yourself when facing Grief. I've experienced a lot of loss in the Grief department throughout my life, and Shad and my Granny Rosie are the only two I'm willing to share publicly. Every day will look different when dealing with Grief: your emotions will be all over the place, and you may feel depressed. But understand that help is there when needed through therapy, loved ones, and friends. Don't hesitate to reach out for an understanding and awareness of the path to conquering Grief.

Entry 31:

The Awakening

The Awakening

I felt like I was sleepwalking through life for a long time. I wasn't living; I forced a smile and hid my pain. Finally, I woke up from a deeply depressed sleep state through the constant dedication to internal healing and rebirthing myself. I wanted my son to experience me: happy, whole, living in my truth & purpose, and not a painful outer shell of myself. I had to return to the "inner child," the mini version of myself, to nurture and heal so that my adult self could guide the way to a better present and future. My internal healing journey began with shame and 360'd into purpose, self-love, understanding, forgiveness, and self-growth.

The talks with the higher power were impactful during my awakening. I spent many hours writing letters to heaven to understand which direction to go, how to heal, how to forgive, and how to revamp myself, including the tools and treatments provided in therapy. And I kept doing the internal work. My Granny Rosie always said: Faith without work is dead. You can't possibly see the transformation for the better in your life without doing the work YOURSELF alongside GOD. But unfortunately, many people start to stumble; some expect GOD to do everything without no assistance from them. WRONG! I kept it transparent throughout this entire read: it's Hard Work that you have to **Assist In** for internal redemption. To get to where you want to be, you must do healthier things you have never done to create a better version of yourself. During my reset process, my son kept me going and still does; I want my son to grow up knowing that it's okay to NOT be okay at times and that healing is the stepping stone toward breaking generational curses. Although we all hate pain, the flip side is that pain instills character development within you that you didn't even know existed. Pain can make one get up when they don't think it's possible. Pain challenges you to navigate through storms to get to the sunshine. Pain Hurts, yet what I've learned on my journey is that it created the motivation to knock down an unhealthy foundation of self to build a transparent, safe, and healthier one. I will repeat Lisa Nichol's affirmation: "I was willing to let the old me die, to rebirth what I am destined to become."

Entry 32:

Protect Your Peace

Protect Your Peace

Every day is a new step in the healing journey for me. I'm still learning, growing, and investing in my purpose of self-healing and happiness. Please don't think you can become magically cured of all pain within a set time frame. Your healing journey will look different from everyone else's because it's YOUR journey. I knew I had embarked on a different level of healing for my journey. I started seeing the positivity within me enhanced; I started paying attention to how my heart is & how it feels, what I'm saying about myself, what energies I'm letting around me, and how I handle situations and people. I BEGAN PROTECTING MY PEACE. When I began to see & feel this, I knew I was headed in a better direction; this is why sharing this open diary with you was important to me because it's scarce that people are transparent about the lows.

For example, everyone on social media shares their highlights, reality shows create a facade of what your life should be like, and even lyrics in some songs peer pressure you to do things that you wouldn't normally do. We are all being conditioned to do something that is not beneficial to our emotional, physical, and mental well-being.

When was the last time you picked up the phone or went in person to see a loved one or friend instead of catching them on social media through a quick like, heart, or comment?

When was the last time you took the phone and technologies away from your kids and yourself and sat, played board games, went outside for some quality time, or just conversated about how each of your days went?

When was the last time you sat and read an excellent fulfilling book that made you forget what time it was?

When was the last time you told someone "I Love You" in person, on FaceTime, or through a phone call, instead of through text messages or DM's?

When was the last time you sat with no distractions, checked in with yourself, checked in with a higher power, and checked in with the universe to see how you were feeling and doing?

If you stumbled on any of the questions I just asked, this is a good stepping stone toward changing the narrative. So I challenge you today to start protecting your peace.

I"m NOT Ready for My Eulogy

I"m NOT Ready for My Eulogy.

I'M NOT READY FOR MY EULOGY!

I GOT A CHILD TO RAISE, UNCONDITIONALLY LOVE, PROTECT, AND SEE GROW UP AND CREATE HIS OWN FAMILY AND SUCCESSES!

I want to know, feel, and experience what it is like to be in love-Real Love.

I want to wear that beautiful wedding gown.

I want to see and experience all my dreams come true.

I want to see, feel, and experience what true happiness inside really does feel like.

I want to be able to live and not just exist finally.

MY EULOGY CAN WAIT!

I shouted this aloud during a recent hospital visit where all my health ailments were attacking me. I cried and screamed; all I could see was my child in my visions. I knew I had to get up and get out of that emergency room.

My team of doctors is fantastic at what they do; they react swiftly and intellectually to help me get back on my feet and get back to my purpose.

It's not easy, though; there are times that they even scratch their heads trying to figure out how to help me navigate all of these health ailments. And it can be emotionally taxing at times for us all. But, what remains a constant motivation for me is knowing that my support team makes sure that I don't ever feel alone- which is most important.

Healing is still a journey, and I am willing to continue to do the work to accomplish every level of internal healing possible. I've come so far and seen so much progress through every tool, treatment, and meditation process I've been a part of emotionally, mentally, and physically. What I hope you take from this read is knowing that healing is not pretty, and YOU have to be willing to unpack your past to get to a better and healthier future. Ask yourself, are you ready to Reset?

Love & Light

Martina